The Whole Food Spiralizer Cookbook

Top Mouth Watery Spiralizer Recipes for Your Gluten Free, Paleo, Low Carb and Vegetarian: Recipes to Help You Find a Sustainable Weight Loss Solution.

By

BETTY MOORE

The Whole Food Spiralizer Cookbook

Copyright © 2019 by: BETTY MOORE

ISBN-13: 978-1-950772-49-0
ISBN-10: 1-950772-49-7

All Rights Reserved. No part of this publication may be reproduced in any form or by any means, including scanning, photocopying, or otherwise without prior written permission of the copyright holder.

Disclaimer:

The information provided in this book is designed to provide helpful information on the subjects discussed. The publisher and author are not responsible for any specific health or allergy needs that may require medical supervision and are not liable for any damages or negative consequences from any treatment, action, application or preparation, to any person reading or following the information in this book.

The Whole Food Spiralizer Cookbook

Table of Contents

REASON WHY YOU HAVE TO GET THIS BOOK 6

RULES IN DETERMINING WHETHER OR NOT A VEGETABLE OR FRUIT CAN BE SPIRALIZED OR NOT 6

   The step-by-step guideline on how to spiralize your vegetable or fruit 6

   Vegetable that can give you the best result when spiralized 7

   Vegetables that work best for prepared lunches: 8

THE WHOLE 30 SPIRALIZER RECIPES: TOP 8 MOUTHWATERY LOW CARB RECIPES 10

   Ginger Seared Salmon in Miso Broth with Jalapeno-Scallion Relish and Zucchini Noodles 10

   Chicken and Pesto Zucchini Fettuccine with Tomatoes 12

   Easy Three Bean Zucchini "Macaroni" Salad 14

   The Best Chicken Zucchini Noodle Soup, Ever! 16

   Tofu Scramble with Broccoli Noodles 18

   Shredded Chard, Apple Noodle and Tuna Salad with Lemon Dijon Vinaigrette 20

   Butternut Squash Rice, Sausage, Apple and Pecan Stuffing 22

   Sweet Hot Mustard Brussels Sprout and Apple-Almond Salad 24

TOP 8 MOUTHWATERY GLUTEN FREE RECIPES 26

   Pumpkin Spice Sweet Potato Noodle Waffles 26

   Zucchini Spaghetti Fried Eggs 27

   Spicy Green Harissa Chicken and Golden Beet Noodles 29

   Asian Peanut Zucchini Noodles with Chicken 31

   Tomato Basil Broccoli Noodle and White Bean Salad 33

   Chicken Sausage and Peppers with Sweet Potato "Dirty Rice" 35

   Baked Spanish Egg and Sweet Potato Noodle Bowls 37

   Garlic Sweet Potato Noodles with Pancetta and Baby Spinach 39

TOP 8 MOUTHWATERY VEGETARIAN RECIPES 40

   Vegetarian Sweet Potato Rice & Bean Chili 40

Vegan Creamy Ginger-Coconut Kale Zucchini Spaghetti 42

Vegan Zucchini Noodle Japchae 44

Quinoa-Beet Rice Salad with Veggies and Feta 46

Vegetarian Lemongrass Green Coconut Curry Soup with Zucchini Noodles 48

Zucchini Noodles with Fire Roasted Tomato and Crunchy Almond Pesto 50

Israeli Couscous with Feta-Mint Zucchini Noodles 52

Zucchini Noodle Collard Green Wrap 54

TOP 8 MOUTHWATERY PALEO RECIPES 55

Beet Rice and Strawberry Bacon Salad with Poppy Seed Vinaigrette 55

Chicken and Chickpea Broccoli Noodle Pasta 57

Spicy Chorizo "Micas" with Sweet Potato Noodles 59

Spiralized Paleo Eggs Benedict with Roasted Sweet Potato Noodles, Avocado and Chipotle Hollandaise 61

Shaved Asparagus and Sausage Sweet Potato Noodle Pasta 63

Thai Pork & Peanut Coconut Red Curry with Sweet Potato Rice 64

Foil-Pouch Sweet Potato Noodle Chicken Fajitas 66

Mexican "Sweet Potato Fideos" Soup with Avocado 68

TOP 8 FAST METABOLISM RECIPES 70

Lemon-Dill Zucchini Pasta with Shrimp and Capers 70

Mint Pesto Zucchini Pasta with Goat Cheese 71

Zucchini Pasta Primavera 72

Lobster Tail Fra Diavolo with Zucchini Noodles 74

Grilled Tomatoes and Basil Zucchini Noodles with Balsamic Glaze 75

Creamy BLT Zucchini Pasta 77

Lemon Ricotta Zucchini Pasta with Kalamata Olives 79

Spicy Parmesan-Garlic Zucchini Pasta with Sausage and Kalettes 80

11 HEALTHY PASTA ALTERNATIVE 82

Cheesy Zucchini Quinoa Bake 82

Pumpkin Spice Sweet Potato Noodle Waffles (Gluten-Free) 83

Tomato Sweet Potato Noodles with Roasted Artichokes and Chicken 84

Raw Pasta Salad with Creamy Lemon & Herb Dressing 86

Zucchini Spaghetti with Easy Lentil Marinara 87

Zucchini Noodles (Zoodles) with Lemon-Garlic Spicy Shrimp 89

Zucchini Noodles with Pesto & Roasted Tomatoes 91

Butternut Squash Noodles with Sweet Potato & Greens 92

Sweet Potato Noodles with "Creamy" Sundried Tomato Sauce 93

Raw Avocado Kale Pesto with Zucchini Noodles 95

Raw Butternut Squash Pasta with Orange Pomegranate Sauce 96

FREE BONUS TUTORIAL: VIDEO LINK ON HOW TO BEST SPIRALIZE YOUR VEGETABLES 97

CONCLUSION 98

The Whole Food Spiralizer Cookbook

REASON WHY YOU HAVE TO GET THIS BOOK

Spiralizing is an effective way of turning vegetables and fruits into noodles. Simple. Spiralized or "*Inspiralized*" vegetable pasta is inherently paleo, gluten-free, vegan and low carb friendly, vegetarian friendly, and of course, it's a cleaner, more wholesome way to eat.

Spiralized pasta is easy to make and it also nutritious and filling. Nevertheless, spiralizing is meant for all ages, skill levels and diet lifestyles. The spiralizer enables you to transform a healthy, low-calorie, low-carb vegetable into a giant bowl of pasta and top with the right sauce and protein and with the snap of the hand you've got a delicious meal that won't break the diet bank.

The major reason for spiralizing, spiralized vegetables are mostly light in carbs, calories, fat and sugar. Spiralizing enable you to eat more vegetables naturally without even noticing (especially when they're well covered in a delicious tomato basil sauce!) This small shift in the way you eat will trigger your weight loss, because you're consuming more vegetables and less processed foods while still remaining satisfied.

RULES IN DETERMINING WHETHER OR NOT A VEGETABLE OR FRUIT CAN BE SPIRALIZED OR NOT

First, the vegetable cannot be hollow, seeded or have a tough core.

Secondly, the vegetable must be at least 1.5" in diameter for best experience.

Thirdly, the vegetable should be at least 2" long for best experience.

Finally, the vegetable must have a firm, solid flesh (make sure it has no squishy, juicy fruits or veggies.)

The step-by-step guideline on how to spiralize your vegetable or fruit

1st stage:

Preparation stage: Preparation of the vegetable or fruit.

1. First, you slice the ends of the vegetable or fruit off flatly and evenly.

2. After that, you peel it (if applicable.)
3. Then you slice the vegetable or fruit in half, if it's larger than 6" long, for best leverage.

2nd stage

1. This is The Stage Where You Use the Noodle Twister to choose your desired noodle shape
2. Remember, the blades on The Noodle Twister are clearly labeled as A, B, C, D.
3. You should simply pull and turn The Noodle Twister (the green knob) to select the noodle shape you prefer.

Stage 3:

1. At this point, you place the vegetable or fruit on the Inspiralizer after you must have align the center of one end of the vegetable or fruit with the central coring blade.
2. After which you press firmly to secure the teeth of the handle into the opposite end.
3. Be certain that the vegetable or fruit is securely attached before spiralizing.

Stage 4:

SPIRALIZED:

1. First, you grasp the side handle for leverage and then grasp the turning handle (with the teeth.)
2. If you want to spiralize, spin clockwise, applying pressure towards the blades.
3. Then you relax and watch the vegetable or fruit instantly turn into noodles!

Vegetable that can give you the best result when spiralized

Courgette

this vegetable will make you forget about spaghetti. You should use the thin noodle attachment on the spiralizer to create long twirls of pasta-like vegetable noodles. This you do by simply boiling the spiralised courgette for about 20 seconds, then top with Bolognese or stir through pesto and some prawns.

Carrots

it exciting to know that the raw carrot ribbons, made with the slicing blade, add texture and crunch to a salad or slaw. Or better still you can stir-fry the carrot ribbons for a couple of minutes with garlic and coconut oil for a healthy side dish.

Sweet potato

You can use the thicker noodle blade to create sweet potato curly fries, all you have to do is toss in a little oil and bake until crisp.

Apples

Remember, coleslaw will never be the same again, add texture with apple noodles; and make sure you toss in lemon juice as soon as the apple noodles come out of the spiralizer to prevent them from browning.

Mooli

This vegetable is known to be part of the radish family and is used widely in Asian cooking. It can be used in place of rice noodles to make pad Thai, or raw in Asian salads.

Vegetables that work best for prepared lunches:

Zucchini and Cucumbers:

When using these vegetables, be certain that the noodles are separate from any sauce or dressing. By separating, all you have to do is avoid excess moisture building up and making a soggy mess. When using zucchini noodles, try adding elements that will soak up that moisture (such as leafy greens – like kale, cheese, etc.)

Apples & Pears:

Remember, fruits such as apple and pears brown quickly and lose their crispness, so I will suggest you avoid spiralizing these in advance unless you're planning on eating the meal that day or you don't mind a little browning and soft fruit noodles.

Kohlrabi, Jicama, Daikon Radishes:

When you using these raw and fitting them into a container, note that they'll snap easily when packed tightly.

Beets:

Remember, beets are messy when it is raw and less messy when cooked, so when packing in advance – keep this in mind and plan accordingly.

Butternut Squash:

Remember, butternut squashes tend to over-soften quickly when cooked – they break up easily and aren't the sturdiest (but are delicious!) try keeping this in mind, in case you had your heart set on a full pasta-like experience for lunch.

THE WHOLE 30 SPIRALIZER RECIPES: TOP 8 MOUTHWATERY LOW CARB RECIPES

Ginger Seared Salmon in Miso Broth with Jalapeno-Scallion Relish and Zucchini Noodles

Ingredients

Ingredients for the salmon:

4 (3oz) pieces of salmon, skinless

2 tablespoons of extra virgin olive oil

2 teaspoons of crushed ginger

Ingredients for the soup:

2-3 cups of low sodium vegetable broth

2 medium/large zucchinis (Blade C, noodles trimmed)

2-3 cups of water

2 tablespoons of miso paste

2 teaspoons of soy sauce

Ingredients for the relish:

2 tablespoons of lime juice

2 tablespoons of finely minced jalapeno (make sure you remove seeds)

6 tablespoons of diced scallions

Directions:

1. First, you place the scallions, jalapeno, and lime juice in a bowl and set aside in the refrigerator.

2. After which you season both sides of the salmon pieces with salt and pepper.
3. After that, you place a large skillet over medium-high heat and add in the olive oil.
4. As soon as oil heats, you add in the crushed ginger, stir and add in the salmon.
5. Then you cook for about 3 minutes, flip over, and cook another 5 minutes or until salmon flakes easily with a fork.
6. At this point, while the salmon is cooking, you place a medium saucepan over high heat, add in the vegetable stock and water, and bring to a boil.
7. As soon as the soup boils, you ladle out about 2/3 cup of the soup into a bowl.
8. Furthermore, you add the miso paste in that bowl and whisk until it dissolves.
9. After which you pour this miso broth back into the saucepan and lower the heat to a high simmer.
10. After that, you add the soy sauce, zucchini noodles and pepper to the soup.
11. This is when you let to cook for 2-3 minutes or until zucchini noodles soften to al dente or your preference.
12. Finally, you ladle the soup into two bowls, add the seared salmon and top with jalapeno-green onion relish.

Nutritional value:

Amount per serving: 2.0serving

Calories: 283

Fat: 19g

Carbohydrate: 9g

Dietary fiber: 3g

Protein: 21g

Chicken and Pesto Zucchini Fettuccine with Tomatoes

Serves: 4

Ingredients

Ingredients for the chicken and pasta:

Salt and pepper (to taste)

¼ teaspoon of dried oregano

1 cup of cherry tomatoes (halved)

5-6 medium zucchinis (Blade B)

1 pound of boneless chicken breast (cubed)

½ teaspoon of garlic powder

Pinches of red pepper flakes

However, this is specific to the Inspiralizer. If you don't have the Inspiralizer, feel free to use a thicker noodle blade.

Ingredients for the pesto:

2 cups of basil (packed)

3 tablespoons of extra virgin olive oil

Salt and pepper (to taste)

2 tablespoons of pine nuts

2 tablespoons of parmesan cheese

1 large garlic clove

Directions:

1. First, you place a large skillet over medium heat and add in the olive oil.
2. As soon as oil heats, you add in the chicken and season with pepper, salt, garlic powder, oregano and red pepper flakes.

3. After which you cover and cook for about 5-7 minutes until chicken is cooked through and no longer pink on the inside.
4. After that, halfway through, add in the tomatoes.
5. At this point, while the chicken is cooking, you prepare the pesto: add all ingredients into a food processor and pulse until creamy.
6. Furthermore, you transfer the chicken to a plate when finished, leaving the juices in the pan.
7. Add in the zucchini noodles immediately and toss for about 3-5 minutes or until cooked to your preference.
8. Finally, you drain the zucchini noodles in a colander and then add to a mixing bowl and add in the pesto, chicken and tomatoes.
9. Then you toss together to combine and transfer to a serving bowl or divide into in

Nutritional value:

Amount per serving: 4.0serving

Calories: 358

Fat: 18g

Dietary fiber: 6g

Protein: 34g

Easy Three Bean Zucchini "Macaroni" Salad

Ingredients

Ingredients for the salad:

1 cup of halved cherry tomatoes

¼ cup of red onion (finely chopped)

½ cup of cannellini beans (drained and rinsed)

Tablespoons of fresh chives (finely chopped)

1 large zucchini (or preferably 2 medium zucchinis)

1 orange bell pepper (deseeded and chopped)

½ cup of canned chickpeas (drained and rinsed)

½ cup of red kidney beans (drained and rinsed)

Ingredients for the dressing:

2 tablespoons of lemon juice

1 tablespoon of Dijon mustard

Pepper (to taste)

4 tablespoons of extra virgin olive oil

1 tablespoon of balsamic vinegar

1 teaspoon of garlic (minced)

Directions:

1. First, you slice the zucchinis lengthwise halfway through.
2. After which you spiraled them with Blade C.
3. After that, you toss the zucchini and the rest of the ingredients for the salad into a large mixing bowl.

4. At this point, you combine all of the ingredients for the dressing in a bowl and whisk together.
5. Then you pour over the zucchini salad and toss thoroughly to combine.
6. Make sure you serve immediately or refrigerate for future use.

Nutritional value:

Amount per serving: 7.0serving

Calories: 146

Fat: 8g

Carbohydrate: 15g

Dietary fiber: 4g

Protein: 34g

The Best Chicken Zucchini Noodle Soup, Ever!

Servings: 8 very hearty bowls

Ingredients

2 celery ribs (diced)

2 garlic cloves (minced)

3 teaspoons fresh thyme (or preferably 1 teaspoon dried thyme)

4 chicken thighs (bone-in, about 1.75 pounds)

6 cups chicken broth (low-sodium)

3 medium zucchinis

½ heaping cup diced red onion

1 large carrot (diced)

1 small pinch of red pepper flakes

3 teaspoons fresh oregano (or preferably 1 teaspoon dried oregano)

2 bay leaves

2 cups water

Directions:

1. First, you place a large soup pot over medium heat and add in the celery, onions, carrots, garlic and red pepper flakes.
2. After which you cook for about 3-5 minutes or until vegetables "sweat" and onions are translucent.
3. After that, you add in the thyme and oregano and cook for another 1 minute, stirring frequently.
4. This is when you place in the chicken thighs and bay leaf and pour in the chicken broth, water and cover and let come to a boil.
5. As it starts boiling, you lower to a steady simmer and cook for about 30 minutes and after 30 minutes, remove the chicken and peel off the skin, discard.

6. At this point, you shred the chicken off the bone and set aside, with any juices.
7. Then you place the bones back into the soup pot and simmer for about 10 more minutes, uncovered.
8. Furthermore, while the bones simmer, you slice the zucchinis halfway lengthwise.
9. After that, you spiraled them, using Blade C and then set aside.
10. At this point, you remove the bones and bay leaves and discard.
11. In addition, you add the reserved shredded chicken back to the pot along with the zucchini noodles.
12. Finally, you cook for about 5 minutes or until zucchini is al dente or cooked to your preference.
13. Make sure you serve warm.

Nutritional value:

Amount per serving: 4.0 serving

Calories: 290

Fat: 8g

Carbohydrate: 12g

Dietary fiber: 4g

Protein: 42g

Tofu Scramble with Broccoli Noodles

Ingredients

2 (14oz) block of extra-firm tofu

1 onion (diced)

2 small red bell pepper (finely diced)

2 teaspoons of turmeric

Salt and pepper (to taste)

4 broccoli stems, Blade C (make sure you save florets for future use)

4 tablespoons of extra virgin olive oil

4 cloves of garlic (minced)

2 teaspoons of cumin

Tablespoons of nutritional yeast flakes (it is optional)

Directions:

1. First, you bring a medium pot of water to a boil.
2. As soon as it starts boiling, you add in the broccoli noodles and cook for about 2-3 minutes or until broccoli noodles are al dente.
3. At this point, while the broccoli cooks, you place the tofu on a plate lined with paper towels.
4. Then you use a fork, smash the tofu until it crumbles.
5. After that, blot the top with paper towels to remove as much excess moisture as possible and then set aside.
6. Furthermore, you heat a large skillet over medium heat and add in the olive oil.
7. As soon as oil heats, you add in the onion, garlic and peppers and cook for about 3-5 minutes or until vegetables soften.
8. After which you add in the cumin, stir for about 1 minute and then add in the broccoli noodles, tofu, turmeric and nutritional yeast flakes.
9. Finally, you season with salt and pepper and cook for about 2-3 minutes or until the tofu is heated through.
10. Then you serve warm.

Nutritional value:

Amount per serving: 3.0 serving

Calories: 266

Fat: 18g

Carbohydrate: 14g

Dietary fiber: 5g

Protein: 17g

Shredded Chard, Apple Noodle and Tuna Salad with Lemon Dijon Vinaigrette

Ingredients

2 apples, stem removed (Blade C, noodles trimmed)

Freshly cracked pepper (to taste)

12-14 large chard leaves

½ cup of roughly chopped pecans

2 (5oz) can of tuna in water (drained)

Ingredients for the dressing:

2 tablespoons of water

4 teaspoons of lemon juice

Salt and pepper (to taste)

    1 tablespoon olive oil

2 tablespoons of apple cider vinegar

2 teaspoons of Dijon mustard

2 teaspoons of honey

Ingredients:

1. First, you place all of the ingredients for the dressing into a bowl and whisk until combined.
2. After which you set aside.
3. After that, you lay out the chard leaves.
4. This is when you cut out the thick stem and stack the leaves.
5. At this point, you roll the stack up into a cigar and cut into thin ribbons to "shred" the chard.
6. Furthermore, you combine the chard, apple and pecans in a large mixing bowl.
7. After which you add in the dressing, saving about two teaspoons.

8. Then you toss to combine fully and then divide into 4 plates.
9. In addition, you top the plates equally with tuna and drizzle the remaining vinaigrette onto the tuna.
10. Finally, you season with cracked pepper.

Nutritional value:

Amount per serving: 1 serving size

Calories: 262

Fat: 13g

Carbohydrate: 16g

Dietary fiber: 4g

Protein: 21g

The Whole Food Spiralizer Cookbook

Butternut Squash Rice, Sausage, Apple and Pecan Stuffing
Ingredients

2 tablespoons of extra virgin olive oil

6 celery ribs (diced)

4 teaspoons of dried thyme

1 ½ cups of roughly chopped pecans

4 tablespoons of chopped parsley

1 cup of shredded parmesan cheese (it is optional)

2 large butternut squash (peeled, Blade C)

6 garlic cloves (minced)

1 cup of diced yellow or better still white onion

6 sweet Italian sausage links (deceased)

2 Gala apple (Blade B)

Salt and pepper (to taste)

Directions:

1. Meanwhile, you heat the oven to 400 degrees.
2. After which you place the butternut squash noodles into a food processor.
3. After that, you pulse until rice-like.
4. Then you set aside.
5. At this point, you place a large, deep skillet over medium heat and add in the olive oil.
6. Immediately the oil heats, you add in the garlic, onion, celery, thyme and season with salt and pepper.
7. After which you cook for about 3-5 minutes or until the vegetables soften and then add in the sausage, breaking it up with a wooden spoon and cook for about 5 more minutes until it's no longer pink.
8. In addition, you add in the apples, butternut squash rice and parsley.
9. After that, you season with salt and pepper and stir to combine.

10. Cook for approximately 2-3 minutes or until everything is heated through.
11. This is when you remove from heat and transfer to a large casserole dish.
12. Furthermore, you fold in the pecans, stir once more and then top with the parmesan cheese (it is optional).
13. Finally, you bake for about 15-20 minutes or until butternut squash rice is no longer crunchy.

Nutritional value:

Amount per serving: 1 serving size

Calories: 231

Fat: 16g

Carbohydrate: 6g

Dietary fiber: 15g

Protein: 18g

Sweet Hot Mustard Brussels Sprout and Apple-Almond Salad

Ingredients

Ingredients for the sweet hot mustard:

2 tablespoons of whole-grain mustard

1 teaspoon of sriracha sauce

4 tablespoons of Dijon mustard

1 ½ teaspoon of apple cider vinegar

4 tablespoons honey

Ingredients for the salad:

2 tablespoons of sherry vinegar

Salt and pepper (to taste)

4 Gala red apples (Blade C)

8 shallots (sliced into thin rings)

6 ½ tablespoons of extra virgin olive oil

2 pound Brussels sprouts (trimmed and cut into thirds or quarters)

1 cup of slivered almonds

Directions:

1. However, to make the sweet hot mustard, in a large bowl, I suggest you whisk both mustards, honey, apple cider vinegar and sriracha sauce. Set aside.
2. After which you place a large skillet over medium heat and add in 1 tablespoons of the olive oil.
3. Immediately oil heats, you add in the shallots, season with salt and cover.
4. After that, you let cook for about 3-5 minutes or until lightly caramelized, shaking the pan occasionally.
5. When you done, you remove the shallots with a slotted spoon and into a large bowl with the sherry vinegar, 2 tablespoons of the olive oil, mustard mixture and season with salt and pepper and then set aside.

6. This is when you place the large skillet back over medium-high heat and heat the final two tablespoons of olive oil.
7. When it is heated, you add the Brussels sprouts and season with salt and pepper.
8. In addition, you cover and cook, stirring occasionally, about 8-10 minutes until the sprouts are just tender and lightly browned.
9. Then you transfer to the bowl with the mustard-shallot mixture and add in the almonds and apple noodles and toss.
10. At this point, you arrange on a platter and serve.

Nutritional value:

Amount per serving: 1 serving size

Calories: 184

Fat: 11g

Carbohydrate: 20g

Dietary fiber: 4g

Protein: 4g

TOP 8 MOUTHWATERY GLUTEN FREE RECIPES

Pumpkin Spice Sweet Potato Noodle Waffles
Ingredients

2 teaspoons of pumpkin spice

2 tablespoons of maple syrup or better still more, to preference

2 medium sweet potatoes (peeled, Blade C)

2 medium eggs (beaten)

A Cooking spray

Directions:

1. First, you heat up the waffle iron.
2. After which you place a large skillet over medium heat and coat with cooking spray.
3. After that, you add the sweet potato noodles to the skillet.
4. Then you cook, turning frequently, for about 10 minutes or until noodles have completely softened.
5. In addition, you add the noodles into a bowl and add in the pumpkin spice.
6. This is when you mix to combine thoroughly.
7. Then you add in the full egg and toss to combine.
8. At this point, you spray the waffle iron with cooking spray and pack in the noodles.
9. Furthermore, you may have to play around with the noodles to get them to fit in all of the grooves.
10. After which you cook the waffle according to the iron's settings.
11. Finally, you serve with maple syrup.

Zucchini Spaghetti Fried Eggs

Ingredients

Ingredients for the pasta:

2 tablespoons of extra virgin olive oil

4 large eggs

4 medium zucchinis (Blade C/D)

2 large garlic clove (minced)

2 small pinch red pepper flakes

Ingredients for the breadcrumbs:

¼ teaspoon of dried oregano flakes

¼ teaspoon of dried parsley flakes

2 teaspoons of water

4 tablespoons of almond meal

¼ teaspoon of dried basil flakes

¼ teaspoon of garlic powder

Salt and pepper (to taste)

Directions:

1. First, you place a medium skillet over medium heat and coat with cooking spray.
2. In the meantime, combine all of the ingredients but the water for the breadcrumbs and whisk together in a small bowl.
3. After which you add in the water and use your hands to form a dough – it should end up in a ball.
4. After that, you crumble the dough ball into the heated skillet and continually break up with a wooden spoon.
5. At this point, you cook for about 2-3 minutes or until breadcrumbs break up, harden and become "toasted."
6. This is when you set aside in a bowl and set the heated skillet to the side.

7. Furthermore, you place a large skillet over medium-high heat and add in the olive oil.
8. As soon as oil heats, you add in the garlic and red pepper flakes and cook for about 30 seconds or until fragrant.
9. After which you add in the zucchini noodles and toss for about 3-5 minutes or until noodles have reached your desired consistency preference (about 3 for al dente.)
10. In the meantime, you place the medium skillet back over medium-high heat and coat with cooking spray.
11. Immediately it is heated (make sure you flick water into the pan and it should sizzle), add in the eggs and cook for about 3-5 minutes or until egg whites set.
12. Finally, you plate the zucchini noodles, top with fried egg and sprinkle over breadcrumbs.

Nutritional value:

Amount per serving: 2.0serving

Calories: 213

Fat: 16g

Carbohydrate: 8g

Dietary fiber: 3g

Protein: 11g

Spicy Green Harissa Chicken and Golden Beet Noodles

Ingredients

6 tablespoons of Mina Harissa Spicy Green Pepper Sauce

2 large shallots (peeled, minced)

4 large golden beets with green tops attached, peeled, Blade C, noodles trimmed and 4 cups of chopped greens reserved

4 teaspoons minced parsley to garnish

2 boneless skinless chicken breast (cubed)

2 large garlic clove (minced)

½ cup of chicken broth

Salt and pepper (to taste)

Directions:

1. First, you place the chicken in a bowl with the harissa sauce and set aside.
2. After which you place a large skillet over medium heat and add in the olive oil.
3. Immediately the oil heats, you add in the garlic and shallots.
4. After that, you let cook for about 30 seconds or until garlic is fragrant.
5. This is when you add in the chicken with sauce and the chicken broth.
6. Then you let cook for 3 minutes or until the sauce thickens.
7. Furthermore, you add in the beet greens, beets and season generously with salt and pepper.
8. At this point, you toss to combine and cover, letting cook for 5 minutes, or until beet noodles are al dente.
9. Then you uncover to toss occasionally.
10. Finally, when it is done, you plate into bowls and top with parsley.

Nutritional value:

Amount per serving: 2.0 serving

Calories: 183

Fat: 2g

Carbohydrate: 12g

Dietary fiber: 3g

Protein: 29g

Asian Peanut Zucchini Noodles with Chicken

Ingredients

Ingredients for the peanut sauce:

4 tablespoons of peanut butter

1 ½ tablespoon of low sodium soy sauce

2 small garlic clove (crushed)

2/3 cup of lower sodium chicken broth

1 ½ tablespoons of honey

2/3 tablespoon of sriracha sauce

2/3 tablespoon of grated fresh ginger

Ingredients for the chicken and veggies:

Salt and pepper (to taste)

1 tablespoon of low sodium soy sauce

4 garlic cloves (crushed)

½ tablespoon of sesame oil

4 medium carrots made into matchsticks (via julienne peeler)

4 medium zucchinis (Blade C, noodles trimmed)

6 springs of fresh cilantro (for garnish)

1 pound boneless, skinless chicken breast (cut into thin strips)

1 tablespoon of sriracha sauce or to taste

Juice of ½ lime

1 tablespoon of grated fresh ginger

1 cup of chopped scallions

2 large broccoli stem (Blade C, noodles trimmed)

2 tablespoons of chopped unsalted roasted peanuts

6 lime wedges

Directions:

1. First, you combine the chicken broth, honey, peanut butter, sriracha, soy sauce, ginger and garlic in a small saucepan.
2. After which you bring to a simmer over medium-low heat and cook, stirring occasionally, for about 8 to 10 minute until the flavors blend and the sauce is slightly thickened.
3. After that, you season the chicken strips with salt and pepper and then transfer it to a large bowl and add the sriracha, lime juice, soy sauce, 2 of the garlic cloves and the ginger.
4. At this point, you heat a large nonstick skillet over high heat and add the sesame oil, then add the chicken.
5. This is when you cook, stirring, until cooked through, for about 2-3 minutes before you transfer to a plate.
6. Then you add the remaining 2 garlic cloves, carrots, the scallions, and broccoli noodles and season with salt.
7. In addition, you cook, stirring, for 1-2 minutes until the vegetables are crisp-tender.
8. After that, you transfer to a plate and add the zucchini noodles to the hot skillet and toss.
9. Then you cook for about 2-3 minutes or until noodles are al dente.
10. This is when you add the cooked veggies, chicken and peanut sauce and cook, tossing everything together, for 1 minute.
11. Finally, you divide the noodles and chicken evenly among 3 bowls.
12. Then you top each with the peanuts and serve with a lime wedge and a sprig of cilantro, for garnish.

Nutritional value:

Amount per serving: 3.0 serving

Calories: 217

Fat: 8g

Carbohydrate: 20g

Dietary fiber: 5g

Protein: 19g

Tomato Basil Broccoli Noodle and White Bean Salad

Ingredients

2 cups of cannellini beans

4 large heads of broccoli with stems

Ingredients for the dressing:

4 tablespoons of minced basil leaves

2 tablespoons of extra virgin olive oil

4 teaspoons of honey

½ teaspoon of red pepper flakes

10-12 Campari tomatoes (seeded and roughly chopped)

4 tablespoons of white balsamic vinegar

2 garlic clove (minced)

4 tablespoons of freshly squeezed lemon juice

Salt and pepper (to taste)

Directions:

1. First, you separate the broccoli florets from their stems and set aside the stems and one head of broccoli's florets.
2. Then, while you will be using both stems, you will only be using one broccoli heads' florets for this recipe (make sure you save the other one for future use.)
3. After that, you remove as much stem as possible from the broccoli florets and place the florets into a food processor and pulse until breadcrumb like.
4. This is when you set broccoli aside in a bowl and wipe down the food processor.
5. Furthermore, you spiraled the broccoli stem, using Blade C.
6. After which you roughly trim the noodles and place in the bowl with the floret crumbs.
7. After that, you place all of the ingredients for the dressing into the food processor and pulse until chunky, but dressing-like (remember do not over process it – you don't want this dressing to be watery).

8. Finally, you pour the dressing into the bowl, add in the beans and toss well to combine thoroughly.
9. Then you serve immediately or let sit in the refrigerator to let flavors marinade.

Nutritional value:

Amount per serving: 3.0 serving

Calories: 198

Fat: 4g

Carbohydrate: 35g

Dietary fiber: 11g

Protein: 12g

The Whole Food Spiralizer Cookbook

Chicken Sausage and Peppers with Sweet Potato "Dirty Rice"

Ingredients

18-20 ounces (about 8 small links) chicken sausages (sliced into ½" chunks)

2 red bell pepper (each chopped into ½" chunks)

4 garlic cloves (minced)

1 cup of chopped red onions

4 tablespoons of tomato paste

2 teaspoons of smoked paprika

Chopped parsley (to garnish)

2 tablespoons of extra virgin olive oil

2 yellow bell pepper (chopped into ½" chunks)

4 medium sweet potatoes (peeled, Blade D)

4 celery ribs (diced)

2 tablespoon + 1 cup chicken broth, low sodium + more if needed

2 teaspoons of dried oregano

Salt and pepper (to taste)

Directions:

1. First, you place a large skillet over medium heat and add in the olive oil.
2. As soon as oil heats, you add in the sausage, peppers and let cook for about 5-7 minutes or until peppers soften and sausage is browned.
3. In the meantime, you place the sweet potato noodles into a food processor and pulse until rice-like and set aside.
4. As soon as the meat is browned, you transfer to a plate with peppers and then let skillet cool down for about 1 minute and then add in the garlic, celery and onions to the skillet.

5. After which you let cook for about 30 seconds and then add in the tablespoon of the chicken broth.
6. After that, you let vegetables cook for about 2-3 minutes or until onions are translucent and then add in the tomato paste.
7. This is when you stir for about 1 minute or until tomato paste coats the vegetables.
8. Furthermore, you add in the sweet potato "rice," oregano and paprika and season with salt and pepper.
9. After that, you stir to combine and let cook for 1 minute.
10. After which you add in the chicken broth, stir again and let cook, covered, for about 5 minutes, uncovering occasionally to stir.
11. Remember if the rice starts to stick to the bottom of the pan, you add more chicken broth by the tablespoon.
12. At this point, you add in the sausage and peppers and cook for another 2-3 minutes, or until sweet potato rice is cooked through.
13. Finally, once done, you add in the parsley, stir to mix and then transfer to a serving bowl or individual bowls and enjoy.

Nutritional value:

Amount per serving: 4.0 serving

Calories: 209

Fat: 10g

Carbohydrate: 22g

Dietary fiber: 4g

Protein: 8g

The Whole Food Spiralizer Cookbook

Baked Spanish Egg and Sweet Potato Noodle Bowls
(1) 6oz ramekin

Ingredients

½ small yellow onion (diced)

2 large garlic cloves (finely minced)

¼ teaspoon of smoked paprika

Salt and pepper (to taste)

4 eggs

Equipment needed: (5) 6oz ramekins

1 tablespoon of extra virgin olive oil

1 jalapeno (seeded and finely chopped)

1 (15oz) can of diced tomatoes

¼ teaspoon of cumin

1 large sweet potato (peeled, Blade C, noodles trimmed)

1 ½ tablespoons of chopped cilantro

Directions:

1. Meanwhile, you heat the oven to a temperature of 375 degrees.
2. After which you take out five 6oz ramekins and set aside.
3. After that, you place a large skillet over medium heat and add in the oil.
4. As soon as oil heats, you add in the chili, onions and garlic and cook for about 3 minutes or until onions are translucent.
5. This is when you add in the paprika, cumin, tomatoes, pepper, salt and sweet potato noodles and cook for about 5-7 minutes or until the tomatoes thicken.

NOTE: The sweet potato noodles might break apart, but that's okay.

6. FURTHERMORE, you portion the mixture into the ramekins and crack an egg in each one.

7. At this point, you season the tops with pepper and bake for about 10-15 minutes or until egg whites are completely set (be careful not to overcook the yolks).
8. Finally, you sprinkle with cilantro and serve.

Nutritional value:

Amount per serving: 5.0 serving

Calories: 133

Fat: 7g

Carbohydrate: 12g

Dietary fiber: 3g

Protein: 6g

Garlic Sweet Potato Noodles with Pancetta and Baby Spinach

Ingredients

2 large garlic clove (minced about 3 teaspoons)

2 pinches of red pepper flakes

2 large (each 350g+) sweet potato (peeled, Blade C)

6-8 packed cups of spinach

2 tablespoons of olive oil

1 cup of diced white onions

1 cup of cubed pancetta

½ cup of chicken broth

8 large basil leaves (chopped)

Directions:

1. First, you place a large skillet over medium heat and add in the olive oil.
2. As soon as the oil heats, add in the garlic, red pepper flakes and onions and cook for about 2 minutes or until onions are translucent.
3. After which you add in the sweet potato noodles and pancetta and season with salt and pepper.
4. After that, you toss to combine and let cook for a few minutes (let say about 2) and then add in the chicken broth and basil.
5. This is when you let it to fully reduce and then cook for about 2-3 minutes or until sweet potato noodles are cooked through (taste to test.).
6. Then towards the end, you add in the baby spinach and let cook for about 2 minutes or until spinach is wilted.
7. When done, divide evenly into bowls.

The Whole Food Spiralizer Cookbook

TOP 8 MOUTHWATERY VEGETARIAN RECIPES

Vegetarian Sweet Potato Rice & Bean Chili

Ingredients

4 large garlic cloves (minced)

4 tablespoons of olive oil

2 cups of diced carrots

2 teaspoons of cumin

1 teaspoon of chili powder

4 cups of low-sodium vegetable broth

4 (28 oz.) cans of diced tomatoes

2 (14oz each) cans of red kidney beans

8-10 avocados (insides cubed)

2 large sweet potatoes (about 340g+), peeled, Blade C

1 ½ cups of diced red onion

2 cups of diced celery

2 cups of diced red bell pepper (or better still green)

2 teaspoons of oregano flakes

Salt and pepper (to taste)

4 cups of water

2 (14oz each) cans of white beans (cannellini)

4 tablespoons of freshly chopped parsley

Directions:

1. First, you place your spiralized sweet potato noodles into a food processor and pulse until made into rice-like bits then you set aside.

2. After that, you place a large saucepan over medium heat and add in the olive oil.
3. As soon as the oil heats, you add in the garlic and let cook for about 30 seconds.
4. After which you add in the onions and cook for 2 minutes or until translucent.
5. Then you add in the celery, carrots, peppers, and season with chili powder, cumin, salt, pepper and oregano.
6. Furthermore, you stir to combine and let cook for 5 minutes, stirring frequently.
7. At this point, you pour in the vegetable broth, tomatoes, water, and beans.
8. After that, you cover, raise heat and bring to a boil.
9. When it starts boiling, you uncover, reduce to a simmer, and stir in the fresh parsley and let cook for about 20 minutes, uncovered.
10. In addition, after 20 minutes, you add in the sweet potato rice, stir to combine and let cook, uncovered for about 10 minutes.
11. As soon as it is done, you ladle into bowls and enjoy garnished with a few avocado chunks (about 1/2 avocado per bowl).

Vegan Creamy Ginger-Coconut Kale Zucchini Spaghetti

One zucchini + ¼ cup of dressing

Ingredients

3 garlic cloves (minced)

One (15 ounce) can of lite coconut milk

Red pepper flakes (to taste)

3 cups of chopped kale

¼ cup of raw cashews

¾ cup of defrosted green peas

½ tablespoon of extra virgin olive oil

2 ½ tablespoons of fresh ginger (peeled and minced)

2 teaspoons of lemon juice

Kosher salt and freshly ground pepper (to taste)

¼ cup of packed fresh basil

6 medium zucchinis (Blade C, noodles trimmed)

Directions:

1. First, you add in the olive oil in a large pot over medium heat.
2. As soon as it is heated, you add the garlic and ginger and cook for approximately 1-2 minutes or until fragrant.
3. After which you add in the lemon juice, coconut milk, red pepper flakes and season with salt and pepper.
4. After that, you stir to combine and then add in the kale.
5. Then you cover and cook for about 5 minutes until the greens have wilted.
6. This is when you transfer the kale mixture to a high-speed blender and add in the basil and cashews.
7. Furthermore, you blend until smooth and creamy and set aside.
8. After that, you wipe down the pot and place back over medium heat.
9. At this point, you add in the zucchini noodles and peas and toss for about 3-4 minutes or until cooked to al dente or your preference.

10. Finally, once it is cooked, divide into bowls and top with green sauce.
11. Make sure you serve immediately.

Nutritional value:

Amount per serving: 2.0 serving

Calories: 159

Fat: 7g

Carbohydrate: 21g

Dietary fiber: 5g

Protein: 8g

Vegan Zucchini Noodle Japchae

Ingredients

2 tablespoons of extra virgin olive oil (or preferably oil of choice)

1 white onion (thinly sliced)

Toasted sesame seeds, to garnish (about ½ teaspoon)

5 packed cups spinach

2 carrots (peeled, cut into matchsticks and halved)

2 (3.5oz) container shiitake mushrooms, stems removed, tops sliced into ½" pieces

2 large zucchinis (or preferably 4 medium), Blade C

Ingredients for the sauce:

4 teaspoons of honey

1 teaspoon of toasted sesame seeds

2 tablespoons of sesame oil

4 tablespoons of soy sauce

Directions:

1. First, you bring a small pot to a boil.
2. After that, while waiting to boil, you combine all ingredients for the sauce, whisk together and set aside.
3. As soon as the water boils, you add in the spinach for about 30 seconds or until wilted and then transfer with a slotted spoon to a plate and gently squeeze out excess water then set aside.
4. At this point, you heat a large skillet over medium-heat and once heated, add in the olive oil.
5. As soon as oil heats, you add in the onion, carrots and shiitake mushrooms.
6. Furthermore, you cover and cook for about 5-7 minutes or until mushrooms are wilted and carrots have mostly softened.
7. After which you add in the zucchini noodles and toss for about 2-3 minutes or until zucchini is cooked to al dente.

8. Then you pour the noodle mixture into a colander and toss to let excess moisture drain out.
9. This is when you place the drained noodle mixture back into the skillet and add in the spinach and pour in the sauce.
10. Finally, you toss to combine all the flavors and warm the sauce, about 1 minute.
11. After that, you transfer to plates and garnish with sesame seeds.

Quinoa-Beet Rice Salad with Veggies and Feta

Ingredients

2 ear of corn

1 cup of water

Pepper (to taste)

1 cup of pinto beans

2/3 cup of pitted and halved green manzanilla olives

½ cup of feta cheese

4 tablespoons of fresh lime juice

Salt (to taste)

½ cup of dry quinoa

4 medium beets (peeled, Blade C)

½ cup of cilantro leaves

1 cup of diced red bell pepper

1 avocado (peeled, diced in small cubes)

2 tablespoons of apple cider vinegar

Directions:

1. First, you cover your ear of corn with lightly salted water in a medium saucepan, bring to a boil and cook for about 2 minutes or until corn is easily pierced with a fork.
2. After which you drain into a colander and slice off kernels with a knife, into a bowl and set aside.
3. After that, you place in the dry quinoa with the water in a small saucepan.
4. Then you bring to a boil and then simmer for about 10-15 minutes or until quinoa is fluffy.
5. Furthermore, you add more water by the tablespoon if quinoa sticks to the bottom before its done cooking and set aside once done.

6. After that, you place your beet noodles in a food processor and pulse until rice-like.
7. This is when you pour into a large mixing bowl with the cilantro, bell pepper, avocado, feta, beans, olives, apple cider vinegar and lime juice.
8. Finally, you season with salt and pepper and toss everything to combine thoroughly.
9. Then you transfer to a serving bowl and enjoy!

Nutritional value:

Amount per serving: 3.0 serving

Calories: 232

Fat: 10g

Carbohydrate: 30g

Dietary fiber: 7g

Protein: 8g

Vegetarian Lemongrass Green Coconut Curry Soup with Zucchini Noodles

Ingredients

2 lemongrass stalk (diced)

1 teaspoon of minced ginger

2 tablespoons of Thai green curry paste

1 cup of water

4oz snow peas

2/3 cup of diced scallions

2 tablespoons of freshly squeezed lime juice

Salt and pepper (to taste)

2 tablespoons of extra virgin olive oil (or preferably virgin coconut oil)

2 garlic clove (minced)

2 pinch red pepper flakes

4 cups of vegetable broth

3 oz. mushrooms of choice (likely 2 large handful)

4oz baby bok choy (chopped in 3" pieces)

1 cup of small-cubed tofu

2 large zucchinis (or better still 4 medium zucchinis, Blade C)

Directions:

1. First, you heat oil in a medium saucepan over medium heat.
2. After which you add in the lemongrass, ginger, garlic, red pepper flakes and green curry paste.
3. After that, you cook for about 2 minutes until fragrant.
4. Then you add the broth and water and bring to a boil.
5. As soon as it starts boiling, you add in the mushrooms, bok choy, snow peas, scallions, lime juice, tofu and zucchini noodles.

6. Furthermore, you let cook for about 3-4 minutes or until vegetables are tender.
7. As soon as it is tender, you add in the cilantro, season generously with salt and pepper and stir to combine.
8. Make sure you serve into bowls.

Nutritional value:

Amount per serving: 1 serving size

Calories: 168

Fat: 12.9g

Carbohydrate: 10.7g

Dietary fiber: 1.3g

Protein: 4.6g

Zucchini Noodles with Fire Roasted Tomato and Crunchy Almond Pesto

Ingredients

For the pasta:

Four medium zucchinis (peeled, Blade C)

For the pesto sauce:

1/4 cup of extra-virgin olive oil

½ cup of fresh basil leaves

¼ cup of freshly grated Parmesan cheese

1 small pinch crushed red pepper flakes

¼ cup of slivered almonds

14 ounces, can diced fire-roasted tomatoes (drained)

3 teaspoons of red wine vinegar

Salt (to taste)

Directions:

1. First, you place a large skillet over medium-high heat and once heated, add in the almonds, stirring frequently, for about 3-5 minutes until golden and fragrant.
2. After which you allow them to cool slightly.
3. After that, you transfer the almonds to a food processor and process until ground into chunks.
4. This is when you set aside in a small bowl and then, in the same food processor, add in the olive oil, basil, tomatoes, and cheese, and vinegar, salt and crushed red pepper.
5. Then you pulse until creamy, add in the almonds and then pulse lightly until combined.
6. However, if you'd like to have this raw: just serve zucchini noodles, topped with pesto sauce!
7. In the other hand, if you'd like to have this cooked: I suggest you place a medium pot over medium-high heat and add in the pesto.

8. Furthermore, you cook the pesto, stirring occasionally, for about 3-5 minutes until heated through.
9. At this point, while pesto heats, you place a large non-stick skillet over medium-high heat.
10. As soon as it is heated, you coat with cooking spray and add the zucchini noodles.
11. Then you toss until al dente, for about 2-3 minutes, or until cooked to your preference.
12. Finally, you serve the zucchini noodles topped with the pesto sauce.

Israeli Couscous with Feta-Mint Zucchini Noodles

Ingredients

1 cup of uncooked, dry Israeli couscous

1 cup of small cubed feta cheese

2 cups of water

4 small zucchinis

4 tablespoons of coarsely chopped fresh mint leaves

Ingredients for the dressing:

2 tablespoons of apple cider vinegar

4 teaspoons of honey

Salt and pepper (to taste)

4 tablespoons of extra virgin olive oil

2 tablespoons of fresh lemon juice

1 teaspoon of grated lemon zest

Directions:

1. First, you bring 2 cups of lightly salted water to a boil in a large saucepan.
2. After which you add in the couscous and cook for about 10 minutes or according to package instructions, until tender.
3. After that, you drain and place in a large mixing bowl.
4. Then while couscous is cooking, spiraled the zucchinis, using Blade A.
5. This is when, you trim the noodles and set aside.
6. At this point, while couscous is cooking, in a small bowl, mix together the ingredients for the dressing and season with salt and pepper then set aside.
7. Furthermore, you place a large skillet over medium heat and add in the zucchini noodles.
8. After which you let cook for about 2-3 minutes or until softened, heated and cooked to your preference.
9. After that, you pour the cooked zucchini into the large mixing bowl and add in the mint and feta.

10. Finally, you pour in the dressing and toss to combine.
11. Make sure you serve immediately.

Zucchini Noodle Collard Green Wrap

Ingredients

4 tablespoons of hummus

8-10 thin slices of red onion

1 cup of zucchini noodles

2 large collards green leaf

    8-10 thin slices of cucumber

6-8 thin slices of avocado

½ cup of alfalfa sprouts

Directions:

1. First, you lay down a collard green leaf.
2. After which you slice the tough stem off the bottom and discard.
3. After that, you spread out the hummus on the leaf with the back of a spoon or a knife.
4. Then you top with cucumber slices, then onion slices and then avocado slices.
5. Furthermore, you top with sprouts and then top with zucchini noodles.
6. Finally, pinching in the sides as you go, roll the burrito tightly.
7. This is when you pierce with toothpicks, cut in half and enjoy.

The Whole Food Spiralizer Cookbook

TOP 8 MOUTHWATERY PALEO RECIPES

Beet Rice and Strawberry Bacon Salad with Poppy Seed Vinaigrette

Ingredients

4 large eggs

14 hulled and quartered strawberries

8 small radishes (Blade C)

8 pieces of bacon

2 large beets (peeled, Blade C)

½ cup of slivered almonds

Ingredients for the vinaigrette:

2 tablespoons of honey

5 tablespoons of extra virgin olive oil

Salt and pepper (to taste)

6 tablespoons of apple cider vinegar

3 teaspoons of poppy seeds

2 teaspoons of Dijon mustard

Directions:

1. First, you place a large skillet over medium heat.
2. After which you coat with cooking spray and add in the bacon.
3. After that, you cook for about 3 minutes and then flip over, cook for another 3-5 minutes or until crispy.
4. Then you transfer to a paper towel lined plate, crumble and set aside.
5. At this point, while bacon is cooking, you place the eggs in a small pot and cover with water.
6. Furthermore, you bring to a boil and then turn off the heat and let stand for about 10-12 minutes.

7. After which you drain into a colander and place the eggs in a bowl of cold water.
8. This is when you let cool for about 2 minutes or until easier to handle and peel the eggs.
9. Then you remove yolks and chop (or better still include yolks - your preference!). Separate and then set aside.
10. In addition, you place the beet noodles into a food processor and pulse until rice-like after which you set aside.
11. After that, you place all of the ingredients for the vinaigrette into a bowl and whisk to combine then set aside.
12. Finally, you divide the beet rice evenly into bowls and top each equally with strawberries, egg, bacon, radishes, and almonds.
13. Then drizzle with poppy seed vinaigrette.

Nutritional value:

Amount per serving: 2.0 serving

Calories: 415

Fat: 28g

Carbohydrate: 19g

Dietary fiber: 4g

Protein: 12g

Chicken and Chickpea Broccoli Noodle Pasta

Ingredients

10 tablespoons of extra virgin olive oil

2 boneless chicken breast

Salt and pepper (to taste)

½ teaspoon of dried oregano flakes

4 broccoli stems (Blade C)

1 cup of canned chickpeas (drained and rinsed)

1 cup of cooked green peas

1 cup of thinly sliced leeks

Ingredients for the dressing:

2/3 cup of feta

2 tablespoons of lemon juice

2 tablespoons of olive oil

2 small garlic clove (minced)

4 tablespoons basil (chopped)

1 shallot (chopped)

Salt and pepper (to taste)

2 tablespoons of red wine vinegar

Directions:

1. First, you place a large skillet over medium heat and add in the olive oil.
2. In the meantime, you season chicken with salt, pepper and oregano on both sides.
3. As soon as the oil starts shimmering, you add in the chicken and cook until no longer pink then set aside.

4. After which you place a medium pot filled halfway with water over high heat and bring to a boil.
5. As soon as it starts boiling, you add in the broccoli noodles and peas.
6. Cook for about 2-3 minutes or until the broccoli noodles are softened and cooked to al dente and the peas are bright green.
7. At this point, you drain and set aside.
8. After that, while broccoli noodles are chilling, you place all of the ingredients for the feta dressing into a food processor and pulse until creamy.
9. Finally, you place the broccoli noodles, peas, chickpeas, leeks and dressing in a large bowl and toss to combine.
10. Then you serve immediately.

Nutritional value:

Amount per serving: 3.0 serving

Calories: 399

Fat: 14g

Carbohydrate: 29g

Dietary fiber: 8g

Protein: 39g

The Whole Food Spiralizer Cookbook

Spicy Chorizo "Micas" with Sweet Potato Noodles

Ingredients

2 large sweet potatoes (peeled, Blade C, noodles trimmed)

Salt and pepper (to taste)

2 small onion (diced)

4 teaspoons of minced jalapeno (omit spicy if you don't like it)

2 teaspoon oregano

2 tablespoons of chopped cilantro

1 tablespoons of extra virgin olive oil

½ teaspoon of garlic powder

1 pound of chorizo links, deceased (about 2)

2 large red bell pepper (diced)

½ teaspoon of paprika

12 eggs (beaten)

Directions:

1. First, you place a large skillet over medium heat and add in the olive oil.
2. As soon as oil heats, you add in the sweet potato noodles and season with garlic powder, salt and pepper.
3. After which you cover and cook, uncovering occasionally to toss, for about 5-7 minutes or until potato noodles are cooked to al dente.
4. After that, you set the noodles aside in three plates and cover (preferably with tinfoil or a plate) and then add the chorizo to the skillet, crumbling with a wooden spoon.
5. Then you cook the chorizo for about 7 minutes until browned.
6. Furthermore, you set aside, using a slotted spoon and immediately add in the onions, bell pepper and jalapeno.
7. After that, you season with oregano, paprika and salt and pepper and cook for about 3 minutes or until vegetables soften.
8. Then you add in the cooked chorizo and the eggs.
9. This is when you cook until the eggs are scrambled.

10. Finally, you divide the chorizo-egg mixture on top of the sweet potato noodles.
11. After which you garnish with cilantro and serve immediately.

Nutritional value:

Amount per serving: 3.0serving

Calories: 424

Fat: 26g

Carbohydrate: 22g

Dietary fiber: 4g

Protein: 24g

The Whole Food Spiralizer Cookbook

Spiralized Paleo Eggs Benedict with Roasted Sweet Potato Noodles, Avocado and Chipotle Hollandaise

Ingredients

Olive oil cooking spray

Salt and pepper (to taste)

2 tablespoons of chopped cilantro

2 large sweet potatoes (Blade C, noodles trimmed)

½ teaspoon of garlic powder

2 avocados (insides cubed)

6 large eggs

Ingredients for the sauce:

Tablespoons of lemon juice

6 tablespoons melted coconut oil

4 eggs yolks

1 teaspoon of sea salt

2 chipotle pepper + 2 teaspoons of adobo sauce (remember, from canned chipotles in adobo sauce)

Directions:

1. Meanwhile, you heat the oven to a temperature 425 degrees.
2. After which you place the sweet potato noodles on a baking sheet, lightly coat with cooking spray and season with garlic powder, salt and pepper.
3. After that, you sprinkle over with the avocado cubes and then roast for about 10-13 minutes or until the sweet potato noodles are cooked to your preference.
4. In the meantime, you place the egg yolks, se salt, chipotle pepper, lemon juice and sauce in a blender and blend for about 10 seconds.
5. At this point, you set the blender on medium and slowly pour in the coconut oil to thicken and as soon as it thickened, set aside.
6. Furthermore, after the hollandaise sauce is made, you fill a medium saucepan halfway with water and bring to a steady simmer.
7. Then you crack the eggs individually into a ramekin or small bowl.

8. This is when you create a gentle whirlpool in the simmering water to help the egg white wrap around the yolk.
9. After which you slowly tip the egg into the water and let cook for three minutes.
10. After that you remove with a slotted spoon and gently rest on a paper towel lined plate.
11. Finally, once the sweet potato noodles and avocado are done, you place like a "nest" on 6 plates.
12. Then you top each with poached (or better still with fried, if you don't feel like poaching!) egg and drizzle with hollandaise sauce.
13. Make sure you serve immediately, garnished with cilantro.

Nutritional value:

Amount per serving: 3.0serving

Calories: 355

Fat: 28g

Carbohydrate: 15g

Dietary fiber: 5g

Protein: 10g

The Whole Food Spiralizer Cookbook

Shaved Asparagus and Sausage Sweet Potato Noodle Pasta

Ingredients

4 sweet Italian sausage links, deceased, crumbled

Salt and pepper (to taste)

½ teaspoon of red pepper flakes

4 tablespoons of freshly chopped parsley

Grated parmigiana reggiano cheese, to garnish (it is optional)

3-4 tablespoons of olive oil

2 large (each 350g+) sweet potato (peeled, Blade C)

2 large garlic clove (minced)

1 cup of low-sodium beef broth

12 asparagus stalks

Directions:

1. First, you place a large skillet over medium heat and add in the olive oil.
2. After which you add in the sausage and cook for about 5-7 minutes the sausage until browned.
3. After that, you continue to crumble the sausage as it cooks.
4. At this point, while the sausage is cooking, snap the bottoms off the asparagus and then shave with a vegetable peeler, starting from the bottom of the asparagus tips all the way down to the end of the stalk.
5. When you are done shaving, chop off the tips and set aside.
6. This is when you set aside all shavings and tips and when the sausage is done, add in the garlic, sweet potato noodles, red pepper flakes and season with salt and pepper.
7. Furthermore, you toss to combine and then add in the broth and parsley.
8. After which you let cook, stirring occasionally, for about 6-8 minutes or until sweet potato noodles are cooked through and soften.
9. Then after about 5 minutes into the noodles cooking, add in the shaved asparagus and asparagus tips.
10. After that, you toss to combine and let the noodles finish cooking.
11. Finally, when pasta is done, plate into bowls and garnish with optional grated cheese.

Thai Pork & Peanut Coconut Red Curry with Sweet Potato Rice

Ingredients

2 garlic clove (minced)

2/3 cup of minced green onions

4 boneless pork tenderloins (sliced into ½-inch strips)

½ cup of Thai red curry paste

½ cup of chicken broth

4 cups of sweet potato rice

2 tablespoons of coconut oil (or preferably vegetable oil)

½ teaspoon of minced ginger

2 red bell pepper (sliced into strips)

½ cup of peanut butter

2 cans of coconut milk

2 tablespoons of fresh cilantro leaves

Directions:

1. First, you place a large skillet over medium heat and add in the oil.
2. After which you add in the garlic and ginger and cook for about 30 seconds.
3. After that, you add in the onions and let cook for 1 minute and then add in the pork slices.
4. Then you cook the pork for about 5 minutes until it starts to brown.
5. At this point, you remove the pork and add in the red bell pepper slices.
6. This is when you let cook for about 3 minutes and then put the pork back into the skillet.
7. Furthermore, you add in the peanut butter and curry paste.
8. After which you stir to combine and then add in the coconut milk and chicken broth.
9. After that, you toss to combine, cover the skillet and let simmer for about 10 minutes, stirring occasionally.
10. Then after 10 minutes, uncover and let simmer for about 5 more minutes.

11. As soon as it is done, you remove the cover and stir in the cilantro.
12. Finally, you remove from heat and transfer to a serving bowl.
13. Make sure you serve alongside the sweet potato rice.
14. Enjoy!

Notes

1. Remember, to make the sweet potato rice, spiraled a large sweet potato (peel first).
2. After which you place the noodles into a food processor and pulse until made into rice-like bits.
3. After that, you place in a large skillet with 1 cup chicken broth and let simmer for about 5-7 minutes or until sweet potato fluffs up and softens like rice.

NUTRITIONAL FACT

Fat: 13g

Carbohydrate: 16g

Dietary fiber: 4g

Protein: 21g

Foil-Pouch Sweet Potato Noodle Chicken Fajitas

Ingredients

Ingredients for fajita mix:

2 teaspoons of chili powder

1 teaspoon of paprika

1 teaspoon of onion powder

½ teaspoon of oregano

½ teaspoon of cayenne pepper

½ teaspoon of garlic powder

1 teaspoon of smoked paprika

½ teaspoon of cumin

1 teaspoon of salt

Ingredients for the rest:

2 yellow bell pepper (sliced)

1 large red or preferably white onion, sliced into ½ inch strips

Juice of 2 lime

2 large (each 350g+) sweet potato (peeled, Blade C)

16 chicken breast tenderloins (or preferably 4 chicken breasts, cut into 16 tenderloin strips)

2 green bell pepper (sliced)

4 tablespoons of olive oil

2 avocadoes (insides cubed)

Directions:

1. Meanwhile, you heat the oven to a temperature of 375 degrees.
2. After which you place a large skillet over medium heat and coat with cooking spray.

3. After that, you add in the chicken and cook for about 2 minutes, flip and cook another 2 minutes.
4. Then you set aside the cooked chicken on a plate.
5. At this point, you combine all of the ingredients for the fajita mix in a bowl and then set aside.
6. Furthermore, you place in the bell peppers, cooked chicken, avocado, olive oil and lime juice in another bowl.
7. After which you toss to combine.
8. After that, you add 2 tablespoons of the fajita mix seasonings to the bowl and toss to combine and then set aside.
9. In addition, you take out a large piece of tinfoil and place the sweet potato noodles in the center.
10. This is when you top with the fajita contents and close the contents by folding the tinfoil into a pouch-like packet.
11. Make sure you leave about 1 inch on the top, when enclosing (for the warm air to circulate and steam the contents).
12. Finally, you place the foil pouch on a baking tray and bake in the oven for about 20-25 minutes.
13. After which you serve in pouches or pour out onto plates.
14. Enjoy!

Notes

Remember, this makes more seasoning than you need and make sure you save the leftovers for another meal!

Mexican "Sweet Potato Fideos" Soup with Avocado

Ingredients

2 garlic clove (minced)

2 (14oz) can diced tomatoes

2 tablespoons of chili powder

2 large (each 320g+) sweet potato (peeled, Blade C)

2 avocadoes (insides cubed)

2 tablespoons of olive oil

1 yellow onion (diced)

1 teaspoon of cumin

6 cups of vegetable broth (low-sodium)

3 tablespoons of chopped cilantro

Directions:

1. First, you place a large saucepan over medium heat and add in the olive oil.
2. As soon as the oil heats, you add in the garlic and let cook for about 30 seconds.
3. After which you add in the diced onion and let cook for about 2 minutes.
4. After that, you add in the diced cumin, tomatoes, chili powder and season with salt and pepper.
5. This is when you let the tomatoes cook for about 2-3 minutes to absorb the flavors of the seasonings and then add in the chicken broth.
6. At this point, you cover, bring to a boil, add in the sweet potato "fideo" and reduce to a simmer.
7. Furthermore, you let cook for about 5-7 minutes or until the sweet potato "fideo" reaches your desired consistency.
8. When it is half-way through cooking, you toss in the chopped cilantro.
9. Finally, once the soup is done, you fold in the avocado.
10. Then you portion into bowls and garnish with remaining chopped cilantro!

Notes

1. However, if you're not a vegetarian, I suggest you use chicken broth - it adds much more flavor.
2. But since we are making fideos, I suggest you slice the sweet potato down the middle into the center (you should be careful not to push the knife all the way through the sweet potato!)

TOP 8 FAST METABOLISM RECIPES

Lemon-Dill Zucchini Pasta with Shrimp and Capers

Ingredients

2 garlic clove (minced)

24 shrimp (deshelled, deveined)

Salt and pepper (to taste)

2 tablespoons of capers

2 tablespoons of extra virgin olive oil

6 roma tomatoes (seeds removed, chopped)

Juice of 2 lemons

4 zucchinis (Blade C)

3 tablespoons of freshly chopped dill

Directions:

1. First, you place a large skillet over medium heat and add in the olive oil.
2. As soon as the oil heats, you add in the garlic and cook for about 30 seconds or until fragrant.
3. After which you add in the shrimp, tomatoes, lemon juice and season with salt and pepper.
4. After that, you let cook for about 5 minutes or until the shrimp are cooked through and opaque.
5. Then you add in the zucchini noodles, dill and capers and toss to combine.
6. At this point, you cook for about 2-3 minutes or until zucchini is al dente.
7. Finally, you divide into bowls and serve.

Mint Pesto Zucchini Pasta with Goat Cheese

Ingredients

1 cup of snow peas

½ cup of crumbled goat cheese (4-6oz)

4 medium zucchinis (Blade C)

1 cup of diced scallions

Ingredients for the pesto:

1 small avocado (peeled, insides cubed)

Zest of 2 small lemon

4 tablespoons of slivered blanched almonds

Salt and pepper (to taste)

4 tablespoons of minced mint leaves

1-2 teaspoons of minced garlic

4 tablespoons of freshly squeezed lemon juice

6 tablespoons of extra virgin olive oil

Directions:

1. First, you place all of the ingredients for the pesto into a food processor and pulse until creamy.
2. After which you taste and adjust, if necessary.
3. After that, you place in the zucchini noodles, snap peas and scallions in a large mixing bowl.
4. Then you pour the dressing over the mixture and toss to combine thoroughly.
5. Finally, you divide the noodle mixture into two bowls and top each equally with goat cheese.

Zucchini Pasta Primavera

Ingredients

2 tablespoons of extra virgin olive oil

½ teaspoon of red pepper flakes (or preferably just a pinch)

1 small red onion (peeled, thinly sliced)

2 bell pepper (seeds and top removed, thinly sliced)

4 tablespoons of freshly chopped parsley

4 medium carrots (peeled and then shaved with a vegetable peeler)

1 cup of grated parmesan cheese (plus more to garnish)

3 cups of broccoli florets

6 teaspoons of minced garlic

2 cups of cherry tomatoes (halved)

1 cup of defrosted green peas

Salt and pepper (to taste)

4 medium zucchinis (Blade C)

4 tablespoons of lemon juice

Directions:

1. First, you bring a medium pot filled halfway with lightly salted water to a boil.
2. After which once it boils, you add in the broccoli and cook for about 2 minutes or until tender but still crunchy.
3. After that, you drain into a colander, pat dry and set aside.
4. At this point, you place a large skillet over medium heat and add in the olive oil.
5. As soon as the oil heats, you add in the garlic, red pepper flakes and onions.
6. Furthermore, you cook the onions for about 2-3 minutes or until translucent.

7. After which you add in the tomatoes, green peas and bell pepper and season with salt and pepper.
8. After that, you cook for about 3 minutes or until the bell pepper softens.
9. Then you add in the carrot shavings, zucchini noodles, lemon juice and parsley and toss for about 2-3 minutes or until the zucchini noodles are al dente.
10. In addition, you add in the broccoli and parmesan cheese and toss completely to spread the cheese.
11. Finally, you plate into bowls and top with additional parmesan cheese, to garnish.

Lobster Tail Fra Diavolo with Zucchini Noodles

Ingredients

4 (4-oz) lobster tails, DE shelled and cut into chunks

4 cloves of garlic (minced)

2 (14.5oz) can San Marzano crushed tomatoes

2 tablespoons of freshly chopped parsley

3 tablespoon of extra virgin olive oil

2 tablespoons of minced shallots

½ teaspoon of red pepper flakes (or preferably more, if you like it spicy)

Salt and pepper (to taste)

Medium zucchinis (Blade C, noodles trimmed)

Directions:

1. First, you heat 2 tablespoons of oil in a large pot over medium heat.
2. As soon as the oil heats, you add in the lobster.
3. After which you cook for about 5-7 minutes until meat is cooked and opaque.
4. Once it is cooked, you transfer to a plate and set aside.
5. After that, you add in the rest of the olive oil, garlic, the shallots, and red pepper flakes to the pot.
6. Then you cook for about 2-3 minutes until onions turn translucent.
7. At this point, you add in the tomatoes, season with salt and pepper and bring to a boil.
8. Furthermore, you reduce heat and simmer for about 15-20 minutes until reduced and thickened.
9. After which you return lobster to the skillet along with the zucchini noodles and cook for another 5 minutes to heat the lobster and cook the noodles to al dente.
10. Finally, once done, you serve the noodles into bowls with even amounts of lobster meat and sprinkle evenly with parsley.

Grilled Tomatoes and Basil Zucchini Noodles with Balsamic Glaze

Ingredients

2 large boneless skinless chicken breast (cubed)

16 pieces of okra (sliced into ½" pieces)

2 large zucchinis (Blade B, noodles trimmed)

2 tablespoons of extra virgin olive oil

Salt and pepper (to taste)

Salt and pepper (to taste)

2 clove of garlic (minced)

Ingredients for the basil pesto:

4 packed cups of basil

6 tablespoons of extra virgin olive oil

½ teaspoon of grinded pepper

6 tablespoons of pine nuts

½ cup of feta cheese

Salt to taste

Directions:

1. First, you combine all of the ingredients for the pesto into a food processor and blend until creamy then set aside.
2. After which you place a large skillet over medium heat and add in the olive oil.
3. As soon as oil heats, you add in the chicken.
4. After that, you cook for about 2-3 minutes or until almost cooked through and then add in the okra and garlic.

5. This is when you season with salt and pepper and cover and cook for about 5-7 minutes or until chicken is fully cooked through, shaking the pan to prevent the garlic from burning.
6. At this point, while mixture is cooking, you combine the zucchini noodles and pesto into a mixing bowl and toss to combine thoroughly, until all noodles are coated in pesto then set aside.
7. Furthermore, when mixture is done cooking, you pour into the bowl with the dressed zucchini noodles and toss to coat thoroughly.
8. Finally, you divide into plates and serve.

Nutritional value:

Amount per serving: 4.0 serving

Calories: 199

Fat: 7g

Carbohydrate: 37g

Dietary fiber: 4g

Protein: 4g

Creamy BLT Zucchini Pasta

Ingredients

2 tablespoons of extra virgin olive oil

½ teaspoon of red pepper flakes

2 teaspoons of tomato paste

Salt and pepper (to taste)

½ cup of grated Parmigiano-Reggiano cheese

8 pieces of bacon

2 garlic clove (minced)

2 (14.5oz) can of crushed tomatoes

1 teaspoon of dried oregano flakes

4 medium zucchinis (Blade C, noodles trimmed)

5-6 cups of arugula

Directions:

1. First, you place a large skillet over medium-high heat and coat with cooking spray.
2. As soon as it heats, you add in the bacon slices and cook for about 2-3 minutes, flip over and cook for another 3-5 minutes or until crispy.
3. After which you set aside on a paper-towel lined plate.
4. After that, you wipe down the skillet and place it back over medium-high heat.
5. Then you add in the olive oil and once heated, add in the garlic and red pepper flakes and cook for about 30 seconds until fragrant.
6. Furthermore, you add in the tomatoes and tomato paste.
7. After which you season with salt and pepper and oregano and let cook for 10 minutes or until sauce is fully reduced.
8. As soon as it reduced, you add in the arugula and zucchini noodles.
9. At this point, you cook, tossing frequently, for about 2-3 minutes or until noodles wilt and cook through.

10. Then you remove from heat and stir in the Parmigiano-Reggiano cheese.
11. Finally, you toss noodle mixture until cheese melts and then crumble in the bacon and give another toss to combine.
12. Then you serve immediately.

Nutritional value:

Amount per serving: 2.0 serving

Calories: 389

Fat: 18g

Carbohydrate: 30g

Dietary fiber: 8g

Protein: 18g

Lemon Ricotta Zucchini Pasta with Kalamata Olives

Ingredients

Zest of 2 small lemon (+ 2 teaspoons of juice)

1 tablespoon of extra virgin olive oil

2 pinches of red pepper flakes

2/3 cup of halved Kalamata olives

1 cup of ricotta cheese

Pepper (to taste)

2 garlic clove (minced)

4 medium zucchinis (Blade A)

Directions:

1. First, you place the ricotta cheese and olives in a large mixing bowl with the lemon zest and juice.
2. After which you season with pepper and set aside.
3. After that, you add in the olive oil in a large skillet.
4. As soon as the oil heats, you add in the garlic and red pepper flakes and cook for about 30 seconds or until fragrant.
5. This is when you add in the zucchini noodles and toss for about 3 minutes or until al dente.
6. At this point, you use pasta tongs to let excess moisture drip dry, transfer the zucchini noodles into the bowl with the ricotta sauce and Kalamata olives.
7. Finally, you toss to combine and then transfer to the pasta bowls using tongs, letting excess moisture drip off.
8. Make sure you serve immediately.

Spicy Parmesan-Garlic Zucchini Pasta with Sausage and Kalettes

Ingredients

4 garlic cloves (minced)

½ teaspoon of red pepper flakes (or preferably less/omit if you don't like spicy)

5 cups of halved kalettes

2/3 cup of grated parmesan cheese (feel free to add more for garnish)

4 spicy Italian sausage links (deceased and sliced into ½" thick chunks)

2/3 cup of diced sweet onion (or preferably red onion)

2 tablespoons of extra virgin olive oil

4 medium zucchinis (Blade C)

Directions:

1. First, you heat a large skillet over medium-high heat.
2. After which you add in the sausage, cooking for about 10-12 minutes or until it browns and cooks completely.
3. After that, you remove the sausage with a slotted spoon and set aside on a plate.
4. Then you add in immediately the garlic, red pepper flakes, onions, olive oil and kalettes.
5. At this point, you let cook for about 2-3 minutes or until kalettes begin to cook.
6. This is when you add in the zucchini pasta and toss for about 2-3 more minutes or until noodles are al dente.
7. Furthermore, you add in the parmesan cheese and sausage and toss until combined and cheese is melted.
8. Finally, you divide into bowls and serve, garnished with additional parmesan, if you so wished.

Nutritional value:

Amount per serving: 2.0 serving

Calories: 464

Fat: 30g

Carbohydrate: 23g

Dietary fiber: 4g

Protein: 27g

11 HEALTHY PASTA ALTERNATIVE

Cheesy Zucchini Quinoa Bake
Ingredients

16 ounces shredded cheddar cheese

4 tablespoons of extra virgin olive oil

4 tablespoons of grated parmesan cheese

8 cups of zucchini noodles (or better still 4 medium zucchini)

2 cups of cooked quinoa

1 teaspoon of salt

Directions:

1. Meanwhile, you heat oven to a temperature of 400 degrees.
2. After which you toss cheddar, zucchini, quinoa, oil and salt together in a bowl then spread into two 8 by 8 baking dish.
3. Then you sprinkle parmesan over the top and bake for about 30 minutes until the top is golden.

Pumpkin Spice Sweet Potato Noodle Waffles (Gluten-Free)

Ingredients

2 teaspoons of pumpkin spice

2 tablespoons of maple syrup or more, to preference

2 medium sweet potato (peeled, Blade C)

2 medium egg (beaten)

Cooking spray

Directions:

1. First, you heat up the waffle iron.
2. After which you place a large skillet over medium heat and coat with cooking spray.
3. After that, you add the sweet potato noodles to the skillet and cook, turning frequently, for approximately 10 minutes or until noodles have completely softened.
4. Then you add the noodles into a bowl and add in the pumpkin spice then mix to combine thoroughly.
5. Furthermore, you add in the full egg and toss to combine.
6. This is when you spray the waffle iron with cooking spray and pack in the noodles.
7. At this point, you may have to play around with the noodles to get them to fit in all of the grooves.
8. Then you cook the waffle according to the iron's settings.
9. Make sure you serve with maple syrup.

Tomato Sweet Potato Noodles with Roasted Artichokes and Chicken

Ingredients

2 boneless chicken breast

2 large garlic clove (minced)

½ cup of red onion (diced)

2 (15oz) can diced tomatoes

Freshly chopped parsley (to garnish)

2 can quartered artichoke hearts

2 tablespoons of olive oil (plus more to drizzle)

2 pinch red pepper flakes (about ½ teaspoon)

2 teaspoons of dried oregano flakes

Salt and pepper (to taste)

2 large (375g+) sweet potato (peeled and spiralized)

Directions:

1. First, you heat the oven to a temperature of 375 degrees.
2. After which on a baking tray, you lay out the artichoke hearts and drizzle with olive oil.
3. After that, you season with salt and pepper and bake for about 30 minutes.
4. After approximately 10 minutes of roasting the artichokes, you place the chicken on a baking tray.
5. Then you drizzle lightly with olive oil and massage into chicken skin.
6. At this point, you season with oregano, salt and pepper.
7. Furthermore, you bake the chicken and artichokes for the remaining 20 minutes.
8. After about 15 minutes, you cut open the chicken breast.
9. NOTE: If the inside meat is no longer pink and juices run clear, that when you know the chicken is done. If not, I suggest you cook for another 5 minutes.

10. After which you pull the chicken into strips and set aside, along with the artichokes.
11. After that, you put the chicken into the oven, then you place a large skillet over medium-low heat.
12. This is when you add in the tablespoons of olive oil.
13. As soon as the oil heats, you add in the garlic and red pepper flakes.
14. After which you let cook for about 30 seconds and then add in the red onion.
15. In addition, you cook the onion for about 2 minutes and then add in the tomatoes, oregano and season with salt and pepper.
16. At this point, you stir to combine and then add in the sweet potato noodles.
17. After that, you toss everything to combine and place a lid on the skillet.
18. After which you cook for 3 minutes, uncover and toss the noodles and then cook for an additional 3-5 minutes or until the sweet potato noodles have reached your desired doneness.
19. As soon as the noodles are done, uncover and add in the done artichokes and chicken.
20. Finally, you toss to combine and plate onto two bowls.
21. Then you garnish with parsley and enjoy!

Nutrition Information

Serving size: ½ Platter

Calories: 397

Fat: 8.2 g

Saturated fat: 1 g

Carbohydrates: 61.2 g

Sugar: 22.5 g

Sodium: 1470 mg

Fiber: 13.2 g

Protein: 24.4 g

Cholesterol: 45 mg

Raw Pasta Salad with Creamy Lemon & Herb Dressing

Ingredients for the Salad:

1 cup of mixed vegetables (broccoli, carrots, cucumber slices, green beans, radishes, tomatoes, peapods, bell peppers, *whatever you have on hand*)

2 zucchini (spiralized)

Optional: 1 cup of protein (diced tofu, edamame, quinoa, garbanzo/white/navy/cannelloni beans, etc.)

Ingredients for the Dressing:

4 – 6 tablespoons of honey (if you want to keep vegan, I suggest you use maple syrup, agave, brown rice syrup)

2 teaspoons of EVOO

1 teaspoon of dill

Pinch salt (optional)

½ cup mayo (regular, soy, Vegenaise, etc.)

2 tablespoons of lemon juice

2 teaspoons of basil (fresh or dried)

1 teaspoon of fresh-ground pepper, or to taste

Stir to combine

Directions:

1. First, you spiralize the zucchini
2. After which you add the diced vegetables and protein.
3. After that, you coat and toss with dressing.
4. Doing this will take 15-20 minutes prior to eating will allow the dressing to soften the noodles and give them a more cooked taste and texture (*Or you simply microwave the entire plate of food for about 30 seconds if you want a "hot meal"*).

Yields: 4 healthy sized plates of food, or 6 more medium sized plates

Zucchini Spaghetti with Easy Lentil Marinara

Ingredients

4 cups of water

2 medium yellow onion (diced)

4 (15 oz.) cans of organic tomato sauce

2 teaspoons of dried oregano

Salt and black pepper (to taste)

2 cups of dried French lentils

4 tablespoons of olive oil (divided)

4 garlic cloves (minced)

2 teaspoons of dried basil

1 teaspoon of dried thyme

12 medium zucchini (spiralized into pasta)

Directions:

1. First, you add lentils and 4 cups of water to a medium pot.
2. After which you bring to a boil and then lower to a simmer and cook about 30 minutes until lentils are tender and liquid is evaporated.
3. At the meanwhile, you add 2 tablespoons of olive oil to a pan over medium heat.
4. After that, you add the onion and sauté for about 5 minutes, or until translucent.
5. Then you add the garlic cloves and sauté for an additional minute, until fragrant.
6. At this point, you add the basil, thyme, tomato sauce, oregano, and salt and pepper to taste.
7. This is when you simmer on low for about 20 minutes.
8. Furthermore, when lentils are done cooking, you add them to the sauce and simmer for an additional 5 - 10 minutes.
9. In a separate pan, you add the remaining tablespoon of olive oil and sauté the zucchini pasta for about 5 - 10 minutes, until a desired tenderness is achieved.

10. Finally, you divide the pasta among four plates and top with lentil marinara.
11. Make sure you serve hot.

Notes:

1. Remember, fresh zucchini will often lose moisture as the zucchini pasta cooks so be sure to drain any liquid that has built up in the pan.

2. It holds well as leftovers, but the zucchini does tend to release extra moisture as it sits so make sure you drain pasta before serving

Zucchini Noodles (Zoodles) with Lemon-Garlic Spicy Shrimp

Servings: 1 Size: 1 zucchini + shrimp

Calories: 235.5

Fat: 9 g

Carb: 14.5 g

Fiber: 4 g

Protein: 25 g

Sugar: 4 g

Ingredients:

Pinch crushed red pepper flakes

4 cloves garlic (sliced thin and divided)

Pinch salt and fresh black pepper

½ cup of halved grape tomatoes

3 teaspoons of olive oil

2 (4 oz.) peeled and deveined shrimp

2 medium zucchini (spiralized)

½ lemon

1. **Directions:**

   First, you heat a medium nonstick skillet over medium-high heat.
2. After which you add 2 teaspoons of the oil and crush red pepper flakes.
3. After that, you add the shrimp and season with pinch salt and pepper.
4. Then you cook for about 2 to 3 minutes and then add half of the garlic and continue cooking for about 1 more minute, or until the shrimp is cooked through and opaque.

5. At this point, you set aside on a dish.
6. Furthermore, you add the remaining 1 teaspoon of oil and garlic to the pan and cook for about 30 seconds then add the zucchini noodles and cook 1 ½ minutes.
7. After that, you add the shrimp and tomatoes to the pan and squeeze the lemon over the dish.
8. Then you remove from heat and serve.

Zucchini Noodles with Pesto & Roasted Tomatoes

Ingredients:

10-14 cherry (or preferably grape tomatoes)

2-4 zucchinis (depending how big they are/how hungry you are)

Ingredients for pesto:

Juice of one small lemon

¼ cup of olive oil (should be very approximate)

2-4 cloves of garlic (chopped)

2 cups of basil (should be approximate)

Avocado (Optional)

Directions:

1. First, you place tomatoes on aluminum foil and drizzle with olive oil.

2. After which you roast the tomatoes at a temperature of 425 degrees for about 20-25 minutes.

3. After that, you prepare the pesto by combining chopped garlic, chopped basil, lemon juice, and olive oil in a blender.

4. NOTE: If you have the Vitamix or better still other high-powered blender, then there is no need to pre-chop.

5. Secondly, if you are finding that the pesto isn't smooth enough to blend, try adding avocado for creaminess (let say about ¼ to ½ of an avocado).

6. As soon as the pesto is prepared, you spiralize the vegetable using your Padron spiralizer.

7. Then you heat some olive oil on a pan on low to medium heat.

8. At this point, you add the zucchini noodles and cook for a few minutes until soft.

9. Finally, you add in the pesto and roasted tomatoes and enjoy!

Butternut Squash Noodles with Sweet Potato & Greens

Ingredients:

Handful of grape tomatoes

½ -1 sweet potato, microwaved (or preferably baked until soft)

Olive oil

2 butternut squash

½ white or yellow onion

2 cups of shredded collard greens

2-4 cloves of garlic

Directions:

1. First, you chop garlic, onions, and tomatoes.
2. After which you peel the butternut squash and chop the bulby part of the squash, put aside.
3. After that, you use the other part to spiralize.
4. Then you heat olive oil in pan.
5. At this point, you add butternut squash and cook for a few minutes, then add rest of ingredients, except the sweet potato.
6. Furthermore, you cook the mixture for a few more minutes until everything is cooked.

NOTE: If it is taking a while for the butternut squash noodles to cook, I suggest you lower heat and cover.

7. Finally, you add already heated sweet potato once the rest is done cooking.
8. Then you toss with olive oil and eat up!

Sweet Potato Noodles with "Creamy" Sundried Tomato Sauce

Note:

Remember, that if you are looking for something more quick and simple, I would suggest you starting off with zucchini with marinara sauce or sweet potato noodles with garlic, olive oil, and parmesan cheese.

Ingredients:

Ingredients for the Sauce:

3 tablespoons of chopped shallots

A few large leaves of basil

White Vinegar

2-4 sweet potatoes (depending on size)
Parmesan cheese (grated for garnish)

½ cup of sundried tomatoes

2 clove garlic (chopped)

Olive Oil

4 spoonful of Greek yogurt

½ white or yellow onion (chopped)

Extra chopped basil (or better still sundried tomatoes for garnish)

Directions:

1. First, you combine ingredients for sauce in blender.

2. After which you taste your mix (NOTE: if it feels too liquidly, you add more sundried tomatoes and shallots. Secondly, if it feels too thick, I suggest you add some white vinegar and/or Greek yogurt).

3. After that, you peel sweet potato and cut in half (NOTE: if it feels too hard to spiralize, I suggest you microwave for 1 minute).

4. At this point, you heat olive oil in pan and add sweet potato noodles.

5. This is when you cook for about 5 minutes (NOTE: If you would like, cover pan to steam noodles to soften).

6. As soon as the noodles are soft, add sauce and toss.

7. Finally, you sprinkle with grated Parmesan cheese and chopped basil.

Raw Avocado Kale Pesto with Zucchini Noodles

Serves 8

Ingredients:

2 cups cherry tomatoes (sliced in half)

4 avocados

½ cup of NUTRITIONAL YEAST (it is optional)

2 small bunch kale, de-stemmed and torn into small pieces (about 2 big handful)

Pinch Himalayan salt and fresh cracked pepper

8 medium zucchini

6-8 cloves of garlic

½ cup of cold pressed olive oil

1 cup of pine nuts (plus some for garnish)

2 tablespoons of lemon juice

Directions:

1. First, you spiralize the zucchini and set aside in a colander to drain excess liquid.
2. After which you start food processor running.
3. This is when you drop cloves of garlic in, one at a time.
4. After that, you add olive oil, avocado, nutritional yeast, pine nuts and lemon juice.
5. Then you pulse until blended.
6. Furthermore, you add kale and pulse until kale is well chopped and incorporated.
7. Finally, you season to taste with salt and pepper, then toss with the zucchini noodles and tomatoes.

Raw Butternut Squash Pasta with Orange Pomegranate Sauce

Note:
This recipe make for sweet yet healthy dinner.

Ingredients:

8 navel oranges (peeled, sliced, and seeds removed)

2 teaspoon of cinnamon

4 to 6 small butternut squash (about 4 to 6 pounds' total)

4 pomegranates (peeled and sliced)

1 ½ teaspoons of nutmeg

Directions:

1. First, you peel squash and slice off ends.
2. After which you spiralize squash starting with thin end. (NOTE: If you do not have a spiralizer, I suggest you use a food processor to grate squash into thin pieces or grate by hand. Remember the texture will resemble more of a coleslaw than a pasta but taste just as delicious.)
3. Then you chop remaining ingredients into fine pieces in a food processor and mix with noodles.

Nutrition Facts

Amount per serving:

Calories: 293

Carbs: 70g

Fat: 2g

Calcium: 190mg

Iron: 2mg

Sodium: 13mg

Fiber: 14g

Protein: 6g

FREE BONUS TUTORIAL: VIDEO LINK ON HOW TO BEST SPIRALIZE YOUR VEGETABLES
https://www.youtube.com/user/GetInspiralized

CONCLUSION

These healthy recipes would help you Shred the Fat Instantly and keep the weight off for good. Get in shape this Season taking this Delectable recipe. If you follow religiously to the

"IT STARTS WITH FOOD" THE WHOLE 30 By MELISSA HARTWIG and some of the

Recipes outlined in this book. You are going to be seeing results in 30 days, because it is proven to work.

The Whole Food Spiralizer Cookbook

www.ingramcontent.com/pod-product-compliance
Lightning Source LLC
Chambersburg PA
CBHW081727100526
44591CB00016B/2536